Contents

Dangerous places...............................4

Desert life......................................6

Desert survival.................................8

Sleighs and sleds.............................10

Cold conditions...............................12

Braving the slopes...........................14

Eating and breathing........................16

Food and fuel.................................18

Warm wool....................................20

Mountain rescue.............................22

Rescue training..............................24

Strong swimmers.............................26

Life-savers....................................28

Glossary......................................30

Useful addresses............................31

Index...32

Dangerous places

Today we are surrounded by computers and machines that can do amazing things. We can launch people into space, explore the deepest oceans and reach the top of the highest mountains.

Antarctica is one of the last wildernesses on earth. People go there to see its beauty and test themselves to the limit.

Modern machines are used to help people cope with extreme conditions: barren deserts or snowy mountain ranges. But in these dangerous places people still rely on the help of animals.

In snow-covered places, such as parts of Norway, travelling by dogsled is common.

Some places are too hot or too cold for machines to work properly. Their engines overheat or seize up, making them useless. But camels cope well both with the heat and the cold, and husky dogs can live and work in freezing conditions.

For the people who live in these places, animals not only provide transport, but a way of life.

This camel is being used to carry wool across the Gobi desert. The ropes are made from the camel's own hair.

A rescuer and his dog search for survivors after a gas explosion destroyed this building

There are some jobs that only animals can manage. A machine cannot easily move across rubble to search for someone trapped underneath. Dogs, however, make excellent searchers.

Desert life

Deserts are harsh, dry places. The people who live there have to bear the cold or fierce heat. The temperature and weather conditions are too extreme for most plants to grow, so deserts are no good for farming.

Desert life is hard. It is impossible to grow enough food to feed even a small community.

Desert people earn their living by trading goods. They rely on their animals — camels and horses — to carry both them and their loads to the different trading posts.

Camels are well-suited to desert life. Their wide-spreading feet prevent them from sinking into the soft sand of deserts such as the Arabian or the Sahara.

Camels' feet are tough and padded. They do not feel the heat of the burning sand.

The Mongols of the Gobi Desert lead a nomadic life, too. As often as 20 times a year they pack up their yurts — the felt tents in which they live — and move to new sites. They need to move on in order to keep trading, to find fresh water supplies and to graze their animals.

The Mongols rely on their horses to help them move their cattle from place to place.

Unlike the Arabian Desert or the Sahara, the Gobi is a mixture of sandy areas and rocky grassland. The Mongols' horses are well-suited to the rocky land. They have strong legs, and their horny hooves protect their feet from the hard ground.

Desert survival

Not only are deserts extremely hot or cold, but in many deserts, less than 10 cm of rain fall each year.

Camels are especially able to cope with dry deserts. Their bodies do not lose water easily — they do not start to sweat until their body temperature reaches 40°C. (At this temperature, we would have a high fever.)

In the hot, barren desert, some camels can survive for up to 17 days without water.

Camels can clamp their noses shut to keep out the sand.

The weather in the desert can change very quickly. Strong winds can whip up the sand into sandstorms. Camels have double rows of thick eyelashes and very hairy ears. These keep sand out of their eyes and ears.

Temperatures in the Gobi Desert reach 45°C in the summer, but in January they drop to -40°C. The Mongols' horses grow a thick winter coat that keeps out the biting desert winds.

Camels, as well as horses, are well-adapted to the extreme cold.

Animal Anecdote

Camels do not store water in their humps, they store fat. When there is little to eat or drink, the animal uses up this fat by changing it into energy or water.

As the fat is used, the hump shrinks, but after a long drink and a meal of thorny plants, the hump soon swells back to its normal size.

A thirsty camel can drink up to 100 litres of water in only a few minutes.

Sleighs and sleds

Not all deserts are hot and sandy. The Arctic is desert too because nothing can grow there. All the water is frozen. Arctic people and animals have to survive extremely cold, and sometimes dangerous, conditions.

Areas of Siberia are also frozen deserts, even in springtime. It is a hostile, harsh environment.

Snowmobiles are quicker than sleds – but their fuel is expensive.

Animals can be more useful than machines in these cold, difficult conditions. Machines, such as snow mobiles, need fuel and are expensive to run.

Travelling by sled is the traditional way to get around in snowy conditions. Instead of wheels, sleds have runners that glide smoothly across ice and snow. The Inuit of northern Canada and Greenland use huskies to pull their sleds. In northern Scandinavia and Siberia some people use tame reindeer.

The reindeer's large, wide hooves allow its feet to spread and get a good grip on the ice.

Reindeer are naturally suited to the cold — they have a thick undercoat of fur and a wiry top coat. Air is trapped between the two layers and keeps the animals warm.

Another advantage of using reindeer is that by the time a reindeer is too old to work, it has usually produced several calves which can be used for work in the future. Old machines, however, may break down and become useless.

Reindeer find their own 'fuel'. They eat grasses in summer and reindeer moss in winter.

Cold conditions

In the snowy wastes of the north, many people keep dogs. The dogs earn their keep by working together as a team to pull sleds or to herd reindeer.

Travelling across moving ice sheets is a dangerous business.

Different breeds of dog are used in the different parts of the Arctic, but they all have a lot in common. Siberian huskies, Samoyeds and Eskimo dogs are all strong, stocky animals. They all have thick fur to keep out the cold.

Dogs are particularly well-suited to the extreme cold. When they get hot they sweat through their mouths. This means the sweat does not freeze on their coats. Frozen fur would cool the dogs down too much; it could make them so cold it would kill them.

In the past, some people ran teams of up to 15 dogs to pull one sled — the dogs would fan out as they ran. Today, they are usually hitched, or tied, in pairs.

Older, more experienced dogs go at the front to show the younger dogs what to do.

Animal Anecdote

Huskies were used by the early polar explorers. In 1911, Robert F. Scott, from Britain, and Roald Amundsen, from Norway, each set out to be the first to reach the South Pole. Both men took dogs to pull their sleds. Huskies were chosen for the expeditions because they can survive in temperatures of -40°C.

Amundsen and his team of four men and 18 dogs won the race.

One of Scott's men, Dimitri, poses with his team of dogs.

13

Braving the slopes

In the high, craggy mountains of the Andes of South America, or in the Himalayas of Central Asia, people live in remote homes, far away from towns or villages. Roads are just rough tracks, so animals rather than cars are used to carry people and their goods.

Although yaks are big, they are nimble so they can walk down narrow tracks.

Animals are also used for heavy farm work. Yaks are big, powerful animals that belong to the ox family. Farmers in the Himalayas mostly use them like oxen, to pull their ploughs.

Llamas are sturdy, strong, animals. They are very useful for carrying small loads over uneven ground. This makes them popular animals in the Andes. But if they are given too much to carry, they simply won't budge!

Caravans, or trails, of llamas are used to carry goods on the high, narrow mountain paths of Bolivia.

Sure-footed animals, such as donkeys and mules, are also often used as transport along narrow mountains paths. Although quite small, they can carry large loads.

Eating and breathing

Living in the high mountains can be as difficult as surviving in the desert. Here, too, temperatures change from very high to very low. These extremes affect the types of plants that grow in mountainous areas.

During winter months, llamas often have to be moved to fresh pastures to get enough to eat.

Animals that live and work in mountain areas must not only survive the weather, but must also be able to survive on the few plants that grow in these often barren places.

Llamas get enough food out of the very rough grasses that grow on the mountain slopes.

Goats are well-known for their ability to eat anything. This makes them a popular animal for mountain farmers. They provide milk, meat, wool and skins in places where there are few other resources.

Goats are often seen on mountain paths, grazing the scrub land.

Animals that live high up are specially suited for their environment in another way, too. Mountain air does not contain as much oxygen as air lower down the slopes. Animals that live in the mountains have big lungs that let them get as much oxygen as possible from the air they breathe.

Yaks can live higher up than any other animals in the world. They can survive at dizzy heights of 6100m.

Food and fuel

In places where the land is poor, people often struggle to make a living. They might only be able to afford to keep one animal – so it is important that this animal can do more than one job.

These women are making cheese from yak's milk. Their tent is woven from yak wool.

Most of the animals that are kept as draught, or pulling, animals also provide food for their owners. Reindeers, camels, yaks, horses and llamas are all mammals – they all produce milk for their young. People can drink this milk, or turn it into butter, cheese or yoghurt.

A foal is held back while its mother is milked. The Mongol family will drink the mare's milk themselves.

In places such as the Sahara Desert, the Arctic Circle, or the Tibetan plains, there are no trees. This means there is no wood to burn, so people use dried animal dung instead. Dung fires keep them warm at night and allow them to cook their food.

Animal dung is dried for extra fuel. It will be burned as well as the wood to see this woman through the winter in the Nepalese mountains.

Animal Anecdote

Mongol riders often travel long distances over barren land. Sometimes their water runs out and they become desperately thirsty. If this happens, they make a little cut on their horse's flank, or side, and sip the blood that trickles out. This keeps the riders going until they reach the next drinking hole, and it doesn't really harm the horses.

19

Warm wool

To cope with the bitter cold, mountain animals have adapted to the weather conditions, by growing long, thick coats. For thousands of years, people have used animal wool and fleeces to keep themselves warm, too.

Camels and llamas have an undercoat that is short and fleecy, to protect them from the cold. This is covered with coarse guard hairs that are waterproof. The undercoat is knitted into jumpers or woven into rugs and cloth.

In Peru, handwoven llama wool blankets are used as baby-carriers. Llama wool hats are ideal to keep children cosy and warm.

Alpacas have much longer, finer hair than llamas. The alpaca's wool is lightweight, strong, warm and water-resistant.

Alpaca wool is used to stuff sleeping bags, or it may be woven with other fibres to make jumpers and suits.

The people of the Andes only shear their llamas and alpacas every other year. This gives the animals time to grow lovely, long coats.

Shearing time is in spring when the weather starts to warm up. When the next winter comes, the animals will have grown back a thick, protective coat.

These alpacas still have their winter coats.

Mountain rescue

Mountains are one of the few remaining wild places on earth. Many people like to go rock-climbing as a way of testing their strength. But in a blizzard or avalanche, even the most experienced climber can get into difficulties.

It is very exhilarating to be at the top of a mountain, but also very dangerous.

Dogs make brilliant rescuers. Because of their powerful sense of smell, they can find people who are buried under metres of snow. Breeds such as Border Collies, Bernese Mountain Dogs and St Bernards are all used for this sort of rescue work.

Bernese Mountain Dogs have a layer of fat and thick fur to protect them from the cold.

Border Collies are part of this rescue team being flown in to search for two missing people.

Today, many mountain rescuers use helicopters. From high in the air, the team have a good view of the land below. But the dogs still have a job to do. They are often taken to where a group of lost climbers were last seen, so that they can pick up the trail from there.

Rescue training

Border Collies are the most popular breed for mountain rescue. They are used in mountain regions around the world.

Trainers often pick out puppies that come from rescue-dog parents. Each puppy goes to live with its handler. Here it is given basic obedience training to teach it how to behave. From the age of 12 months, the dog starts its rescue training.

Border Collies are one of the most intelligent breeds of dog and are easy to train.

The dog is taught to follow the trail of a scented object buried in the snow. When it finds the object, the dog is taught to bark. This tells its handler where it is. The dog is taught to bark when it finds a missing person, too.

If a dog finds someone in the snow, it is taught to dig gently around the person to loosen the snow.

Animal Anecdote

Barry the St Bernard saved the lives of more than 40 people during his 12 years working as a rescue dog in the Swiss Alps.

Barry found one boy half frozen under an avalanche in which his mother died. Barry lay on the boy to keep him warm. The dog licked the boy's face until he woke up.

Strong swimmers

Animals can save us from danger in water, as well as on land. Dogs are sometimes used to rescue swimmers who are in trouble. Their keen senses of sight and hearing help them to spot the person to be rescued.

Animal Anecdote

Jason Page was eight years old when he had a terrifying experience. On holiday with his family, he went off to swim in the sea. Strong currents pulled Jason out of his depth and into trouble. His family could not hear his cries, but his dog Gulliver did. Gulliver swam out to Jason and gently pulled him to safety.

In the United States, a more unusual creature is used to help in the open seas. The American Navy trains dolphins to find torpedoes left over from the Second World War (1939-1945).

Dolphins are well-known for their intelligence and their willingness to help people.

Each dolphin is fitted with a special 'claw' on its snout. It is trained to nudge the claw against the torpedo. The claw fixes to the torpedo and a balloon blows up. This carries the bomb to the surface of the water where it is made safe. The Navy tried using mini-submarines to get the torpedoes back. These were not as good at reaching into tiny cracks on the ocean floor as the dolphins, with their long snouts.

Life-savers

Animals provide life-saving help searching for people after a disaster. After an earthquake, bomb explosion or tornado there is rubble everywhere.

> Some disasters are so bad, it may be necessary to lower help into the area.

Rescue-workers and their sniffer dogs search for victims. With their sensitive noses, dogs can find where people are lying.

Dogs can also be fitted with special computer-linked cameras that show where heat is. Our bodies give off heat when we are alive. As the dogs search the rubble, rescuers check for heat images on the computer in the hope of finding survivors.

> A search through rubble after a tornado struck in Illinois, in the United States.

Animals help us to prevent disasters as well as deal with them. Land mines are bombs that lie in wait for victims long after a war is over. No one knows exactly where they are buried. There are about 110 million buried mines in the world today.

Sniffer dogs are trained to find the mines so that they can be safely exploded by bomb experts.

The dogs are trained to recognise the smell of the gases that the mines give off.

Like the many other animals that help us live and work in dangerous conditions, bomb sniffer dogs are animal heroes who help save many lives.

Glossary

adapted   when something has changed to suit a situation.

Antarctica   ice-covered area of the world, at the South Pole.

Arctic   ice-covered area of the world, at the North Pole.

avalanche   a fast-moving landslide of snow, ice and rock.

barren   where nothing grows; a bare area.

blizzard   a violent snowstorm.

environment   surroundings; everything about a place from the types of plants that grow and the animals that live there to the weather conditions.

harsh   rough, uncomfortable.

mountain range   a chain of mountains that all formed at the same time.

scrub land   land where only a few thorny bushes or dry grasses grow.

torpedo   a tube-shaped bomb that rockets through the water and can be fired from a plane, a ship or a submarine.

Useful addresses

United Kingdom

British Antarctic Survey
High Cross
Madingley Road
Cambridge
CB3 0ET
www.antarctica.ac.uk

Search And Rescue Dog Association (SARDA) - Southern Scotland
3A Bainfield Road
Cardross
Dumbartonshire
G82 5JQ
www.nsarda.org.uk

United States of America

Federal Bureau of Investigation
www.fbi.gov/kids/k5th/kids5th.htm

National Geographic Society
1145 17th Street NW
Washington, DC 20036-4688
www.nationalgeographic.com/animals

Smithsonian National Museum of Natural History
Arctic Studies Center
Department of Anthropology
National Museum of Natural History, Smithsonian Institution
Washington DC 20560-0112
www.mnh.si.edu/arctic/html/wildlife.html

Australia

Melbourne Zoo
PO Box 74
Parkville
Vic. 3052
www.zoo.org.au

Index

alpacas 21
Antarctica 4, 13
Arctic 10, 12, 19
avalanche 22

barren 8, 19
blizzard 22

camels 5, 6, 8, 9, 18, 20
clothing
  animals used for 20, 21

deserts 6, 7, 8, 9, 10,
  16, 19
dogs 4, 5, 11, 12, 13,
  23, 24, 25, 26, 28, 29
dolphins 27
donkeys 15

food
  animals for 17, 18
fuel
  animals for 19

goats 17

harsh environments 6, 10
horses 6, 7, 18, 19
huskies 4, 5, 11, 12, 13

land mines 29
llamas 15, 16, 18, 20, 21

machines 4, 5, 10, 11
Mongols 7, 9, 18, 19
mountain ranges 14, 15,
  16, 19, 21, 22
mountain rescue 23, 24,
  25
mules 15

oxen 14

reindeer 11, 12, 18
rescue animals 5, 23, 24,
  25, 26, 27, 28, 29

sleds 4, 10, 11
sniffer dogs 28, 29

transport
  *animals as 4, 5, 14,
  15, 18, 19*

weather conditions 5, 6
  8, 16, 20
wilderness 4, 22

yaks 14, 17, 18